The Police N[...]

Handbook

Power, Influence, & Persuasion:
How to Get It. How to Use It.

Ronald J. York
President of POLICEPAY.NET, Inc.

POLICEPAY.NET, Inc.
219 West Boyd Street; Suite 205
Norman, Oklahoma 73069

Telephone: (405) 701-8616
Facsimile: (405) 701-8631

E-mail: editor@policepay.net

http://www.policepay.net

The Police Negotiator's Handbook by Ronald J. York
Cover design, editing, and typesetting by Charles L. Wonsey

A POLICEPAY.NET, Inc. Publication

Published by POLICEPAY.NET, Inc.
Printed in the United States of America
First Edition
ISBN: 978-0-6151-5260-8

Acknowledgements

This book was written to assist police union representatives
in collective bargaining by providing a framework from which
to work before, during, and after negotiations. For taking my
manuscript and arriving at the book that you are now holding,
I thank Charles Wonsey for his efforts in the editing and layout
of this book. I also must give thanks to the hundreds of police
unions that have selected me to aide them during negotiations,
allowing me to develop the negotiation methods that I use today
and that I am sharing with you now. While it would be too lengthy
to give individual credit to every client that provided a venue for
developing my current negotiation practices here, I have included a
listing of past and current clients at the back of this text. It has been
a pleasure serving these organizations over the last 20 years and I
look forward to all of the future agencies that I have the priviledge
to assist.

Preface

POLICEPAY.NET, Inc. is a corporation that I formed in 2001. This was done at the same time we launched the POLICEPAY Web site. My personal experience in this area goes back more than twenty years. Prior to 2001, I ran the business through my certified public accounting firm. My first involvement in public safety collective bargaining actually began nearly forty years ago. I was in my early twenties and was starving as I tried to attend college. Someone suggested that I apply with the fire department. Because of their low pay, the department had many vacancies.

As I worked toward my degree in economics and accounting, I became interested in public safety collective bargaining. Unfortunately, there was no collective bargaining law for public safety at that time in Oklahoma. As a result, I became involved with other fire fighters and police officers who were interested in getting collective bargaining rights. Eventually, we drafted such a law, patterned after the New York State Public Employees Fair Employment Act (Taylor Law). We managed to get it passed by the legislature; just to have it vetoed by the governor. That fall, the governor was defeated for reelection. The following winter, we again got the bill through the legislature and the new governor signed it into law.

Several days after the law went into effect, I organized the first public safety bargaining unit under the new provisions – IAFF Local 2041. I was elected president of the new union and immediately began negotiating for a new contract. The only problem was that I had no idea as to what to do. I embarked on the process of trial and error – mostly error. I tried to develop a George Meany/Walter Reuther persona. That bombed. Next, I tried negative radio and newspaper ads. That didn't work either. Eventually, I did get an agreement, although I do not know how.

By the time I had obtained my degree in economics and accounting, went to graduate school, and passed the CPA exam, ten years had gone by since I hired on with the fire department. I had negotiated several contracts during that period. I still did not know much about how to negotiate a contract, but I had certainly discovered many of the wrong things to do.

At that point, I left the fire department and started a CPA practice. At that time, it was illegal for CPA's, attorneys, and doctors to advertise. After starving again for several months, I had an opportunity to purchase a CPA practice from the estate of an older man who had passed away. I made a deal that required no money up front and had five years of monthly payments. This old CPA had the usual tax and bookkeeping clients, but he also had about a dozen small cities that he was providing annual audits to. I worked diligently at this for about ten years.

One day, I received a phone call from one of the police officers who helped get the collective bargaining bill passed. By this time, he had been the president of the Oklahoma City FOP and was currently the national president for the FOP. His name is Dick Boyd. I did not realize at the time what an impact this phone call would make on my life. He said he was helping a police union with contract negotiations, but was getting nowhere because the city claimed it was broke. He said that he had tried to read the city's financial statements but they were completely foreign to him. He asked if I would be willing to look at them. Dick is not one to say no to and he usually wants things in a hurry. It wasn't but a few minutes later that he was at my office with the statements. After looking them over, I soon realized that this city was loaded.

When Dick called later, I told him what I had found. He said that it was just what he had suspected and that there was an arbitration hearing tomorrow that he wanted me to testify at. Immediately, I began to explain why I could not do that. You see, I worked for cities doing audits. If I started working against cites at arbitration hearings, they would all fire me. At that point, Dick told me that if I would testify tomorrow, he would strong-arm enough police unions into using me that I would not need to do city audits. If you know Dick, then you also know that "NO" was not an option. I testified. We won the arbitration award. I got rid of my city audits and embarked on a new journey in my life. It is now more than twenty years later and all that I do today is what most of you know me for. I have worked for police unions as large as the Chicago FOP and as small as a seven man bargaining unit.

I could say that this book is the compilation of all of my wisdom concerning public safety collective bargaining, but that would be a lie. I am still operating by trial and error. The contents of this book are a portion of what is left after having spent forty years learning and eliminating the wrong things to do. Hopefully, this book will help you by teaching you proven techniques and helping you to avoid some of the mistakes that I made when I began negotiating all those years ago.

June, 2007

Table of Contents

Introduction

This publication is called a handbook because it is brief and to the point. It is not, by any stretch of the imagination, the definitive writing on the subject of police contract negotiations. The primary focus is on the negotiations procedures and only slightly touches on technique while completely ignoring theory. I quite possibly could have written a 700-page tome that covered everything I have to say on negotiations. I doubt if many of you would be willing to invest that much time and effort into mastering labor negotiations. If you are interested in learning more, please let me know. I could be convinced to write more on the subject, I think.

Power, influence, and persuasion are all familiar words. Most people believe that they fully understand the meaning of each of these words. In reality, few truly understand how each relates to the other and how each determines the success or failure of contract negotiations. Contract negotiations are like a race car. The engine under the hood represents power. Without it, the car can't do anything at all. Influence is similar to the transmission. The power from the engine won't do much good if we can't harness that power and direct it to where it needs to go. Power is distributed as influence. In our race car, the transmission distributes its influence throughout the drive train and the rear axle causing the tires to move – this is persuasion. As far as negotiations go, you won't be moving any tires, but I can promise you there will be people that you need to move from a nay vote to a yay vote.

To build a winning race car, the most powerful engine should be selected. Next, the correct transmission to harness the power of the engine has to be designed. The transmission is then connected to the rear axle. Finally, persuaded by the influence from the transmission, the axle moves the tires and advances the car around the track. Building a negotiations strategy is the same. First, you must build a power base. Second, it is imperative that you develop a plan to convert that power to influence and to distribute this influence appropriately. Finally, you are ready to take advantage of your influence and to persuade the decision maker to move in the desired direction.

Power is raw energy. Our society holds power in low esteem. Power is seen as a weapon of intimidation and coercion. Most people believe Lord Acton was correct when he said, "Power tends to corrupt; absolute power corrupts absolutely." Lord Acton was wrong. Power is not something to be feared or avoided. Power is a required ingredient for all successful people and organizations. Police unions are constantly trying to limit the power of their police chief. They do so because it is feared that he might misuse that power to deal unfairly with their membership. This fear

is unfounded. It is the powerless chief that should be avoided.
Leaders with limited power become arbitrary and overbearing.
The weak leader sees his authority as constantly being challenged.
To rebuke the attacks, he issues unreasonable orders and directives.
A leader with power does not feel the need to do that.

Influence is raw energy that has been harnessed. For our purposes,
influence can be defined as directing power in a controlled manner
to cause an object (or person) to move. The transmission and
drive shaft of a car do exactly that. Without power, influence is
not possible. Influence is what motivates people to change their
behavior. Influence comes in two forms – reward and punishment.
People lust for reward while fearing punishment. Influence can
sometimes cause unfavorable results. Although it may move
a person, it may not be in the correct direction. In a stand off
situation, the old ultimatum, we have the place surrounded - come
out with your hands up, might cause the person to shoot himself.
That is obviously not the desired outcome.

Persuasion is applying influence to get the correct results.
Persuasion is a combination of the brake pedal, accelerator, and
steering wheel. Power propagates influence. Influence allows
persuasion.

- Power equals public support
- Influence equals key relationships
- Persuasion equals using influence

This handbook is presented in six stages:

Stage One – Research Evidence
Stage Two – Develop an Argument

Stage Three – Create Key Relationships
Stage Four – Generate Public Support
Stage Five – Plan Your Strategy
Stage Six – Negotiate the Deal

It is very important that each stage is done in sequential order.
Each stage is dependent upon the previous stages. Do not skip
any stages! Each stage is presented in a series of steps. Each step
should be followed in sequential order. Do not skip any steps!

As you read through this handbook, it may appear that I am
attacking attorneys. However, I am not. I have no problem with
attorneys. I only have a problem with attorneys that behave
like attorneys during contract negotiations. Actually, some of
the best negotiators I know are attorneys. Some do recognize
and appreciate the differences between the court room and
the negotiating table. Negotiations have nothing to do with law.
Negotiations are about persuasion. If you allow the lawyers to
commandeer the negotiations process, you may as well give up
and take whatever the city offers. If your attorney and the city's
attorney wrestle control of the negotiating process away from you,
they will immediately start playing "lawyerball." Attorneys will
deny this and claim that they have no idea what I am talking about.
This simply isn't true, they know all too well. Once "lawyerball" is
started, there is a metamorphosis from negotiations to a civil lawsuit
process, including all of the lawyers' union (the bar) work rules,
rules they like to call ethics. Don't fall for it.

CHAPTER 1

Stage One:
Research Evidence

It all begins with research. Without the facts and the knowledge
provided by research, there is no basis for an argument. Without
an argument, there is nothing to present. There are seven steps to
research. To skip any of these steps could prove a fatal error. What
kind of research should you do? I am going to explain it in reverse
order. First, we will list the reports that must be generated and what
they should include. It should then become obvious what data you
will need to collect. Each of the seven steps to research result in a
report being generated, these steps include:

1) The turnover report
2) The staffing report
3) The recruitment report
4) The exit interviews report
5) The pay and benefits survey

6) The costing analysis
7) The ability-to-pay study

Step One – The Turnover Report

A turnover report compares the number of employees leaving the department annually to the total employee count. For example, a department with 300 officers that loses 15 officers during a year has a turnover rate of 5 percent (15 divided by 300 or losses divided by total officers). Data should be collected and reported year-by-year for the last 10 years. To make the report even more valuable, separate the controllable and uncontrollable exits. An employee that separates due to retirement, becoming permanently disabled, or death would be considered an uncontrollable exit. Those who quit or get fired prior to retirement are normally considered controllable exits. A firing is usually a bad hiring decision.

Step Two – The Staffing Report

A staffing report compares the actual number of officers to the authorized strength and the city's population. Data should be collected and reported year-by-year for the last 10 years.

Step Three – The Recruitment Report

The recruitment report measures both the quality and quantity of applicants and recruits. The data should be reported on either a year-by-year basis or by academy classes and should include:

1) Total applicants compared to available positions
2) Number surviving initial screening
3) Number surviving entrance exam
4) Number surviving background check
5) Number accepted into academy

6) Number surviving academy
7) Number actually hired
8) Number still employed after first year
9) Number still employed after second year
10) Number still employed after third year
11) Number still employed after fourth year
12) Number still employed after fifth year

The quality portion should include the following:

1) Average education level
2) Average entrance test scores
3) Average age at time of application

Data should be collected and reported year-by-year for the last 10 years. If your department has not tracked this information historically, now is the time to start.

Step Four - The Exit Interviews Report

This report should show why people left and where they went. Include only those who voluntarily resign prior to retirement. Report the following:

1) Number going to other police departments
2) Number going to a career outside of law enforcement
3) Number leaving for something other than a better job
4) Number leaving for better pay
5) Number leaving because of police management
6) Number leaving because they do not like working in law enforcement

Step Five – The Pay and Benefits Survey

The most reliable pay survey is done on a total compensation basis. The survey must include all forms of compensation that can be reasonably measured. The number of hours that have to be worked each year must be computed for an accurate comparison. To arrive at this number, take the number of hours in a normal work week multiplied by 52 and subtract all available paid time off. Do this year-by-year for years 1 through 30.

When subtracting the paid time off, include the following benefits and deduct them from the normal hours worked (typically 2,080 hours):

1) Vacation leave
2) Holiday leave
3) Personal leave
4) Sick leave

Now that you have determined the number of hours an officer is required to work during each year, divide the total compensation value by the total hours worked to arrive at the hourly rate for each hour actually spent on the job. The best point of comparison is obtained by averaging all 30 years, thereby comparing only a single number – the hourly rate for a 30-year career.

When calculating the total compensation value, be certain to include the value of the following benefits:

1) Base pay
2) Longevity
3) Shift differentials
4) Holiday pay
5) Uniform allowance
6) Education pay

7) Pension contribution pickup
8) Employer pension contribution
9) Employer health insurance contribution
10) Employer retiree insurance contribution
11) F.I.C.A. employer contribution

For a valid survey, the agencies included in the survey must be similar departments. Comparability should be based primarily upon size and geographic location. The smaller your department, the closer the comparison sites should be to you geographically. It makes sense for Chicago to compare to New York and Los Angeles because there are not comparably sized cities in their local market. It does not make sense, however, for Peoria to compare with Santa Monica or Yonkers when cities of similar size to Peoria can be located within the same region. Adjustments for the differences in the local cost of living must be made when measuring departments outside of the immediate market. A salary of $50,000 in San Francisco is not the same as a salary of $50,000 in Birmingham. There are several resources for a cost of living index. ACCRA's COLI is the most prevalent.

Once the survey has been compiled, determine where your department should fall in the survey. One agency belongs in first and another should be in last. Not every agency belongs at the average. Typically, larger departments in cities with a higher per capita personal income pay more. This is not always true, but most of the time this relationship is evident.

Step Six – The Costing Analysis

Without knowing the cost of a pay increase, it is difficult to assert that the city can afford it. The best way to calculate the cost of a base pay raise is to use the current operating budget. Do not be concerned with what is budgeted for the current year, but rather what was actually spent last year. Many times, the budgeted amount is greatly inflated because there is no allowance for vacancies. The numbers shown in the audited financial statements are more reliable. Unfortunately, there is seldom enough detail to make the necessary computations. In the budget, there is a column for the prior year. It is usually labeled as "Current Year Estimate." This is because the fiscal year has not yet ended when the budget is prepared. The city takes the expenditures to date and estimates additional spending through year end. This is usually the most accurate data available.

Only calculate the cost of a 1 percent base pay raise. Other amounts can be determined by multiplying the 1 percent value. Start by determining the total annual base pay amount for the ranks covered by the union contract. This should be the base number that all other costs are computed from. For these calculations, only items that are affected by a base pay increase should be included. If the average longevity is 15 percent of base pay, then multiply the total base pay cost by 15 percent. If longevity is stated in flat dollar amounts, e.g. 200 dollars per year, do not include it. The most common "roll up" costs are:

1) Longevity pay
2) Shift pay
3) Holiday pay
4) FICA contributions by the employer
5) Pension contributions by the employer
6) Overtime costs

Everything that will increase as the result of a base pay raise should be measured. Do not include step pay raises. Step pay raises do not increase the total payroll. Step pay raises are offset by savings from retirements and terminations.

Step Seven – The Ability-To-Pay Study

Virtually every city will claim that it cannot afford to increase your pay. Seldom is this actually true. A typical city has a long-term per capita growth rate for revenues that exceeds the long-term growth rate of wages. On the city's side, ability-to-pay could more accurately be called willingness-to-pay. Most cities have the money. They just have a list of priorities that does not rank wages very high.

A person with municipal finance knowledge will be required to prepare this report. It is tempting to skip this report, because it cannot be done in-house. Do not make this mistake. Unless he is taken out, the city's finance director will eliminate any chance of an agreement being obtained. If you can't prove the city's ability-to-pay, the finance guy will certainly be able to produce a report backing up their unwillingness-to-pay.

CHAPTER 2

Stage Two:
Develop an Argument

The argument (the case) is the most important element of the entire
process. Everything from this point forward will be reliant upon
the argument. Do not rush through this stage! The argument has
three components. These components are a result of the first three
steps of developing your argument. The complete process for
developing and articulating your argument is:

1) Identifying the Problem
2) Determining the Cause
3) Specifying the Solution
4) Developing the Message
5) Selecting the Talking Points
6) Writing the Stump Speech

The argument always begins with the problem. It has to be a problem for the city, not the union. The union sees the problem as being overworked and underpaid. This is in no way a problem for the city. The city is apathetic toward the union's problems. The city is concerned with their own problems. The most important being they have limited resources with virtually unlimited needs. You cannot help the city with that problem. Your objective is to get the city to reprioritize its to-do list.

Once the problem has been identified, the cause must be determined. It is difficult to present a solution if the cause is unknown. The solution must modify the cause, thus giving relief from the problem. The solutions to the city's problem and the union's problem have to be the same.

The research from Stage One provides all of the information needed to identify the problem and the cause. The research also indicates the solution. Go through the process, one step at a time.

Step One - The Problem

The problem is the same for every city – recruitment and retention. If a connection between compensation and recruitment and retention cannot be made, there is no way to create a plausible argument. If the city perceives that its needs are being met by the current pay structure, it has no motivation to increase pay. Every product and service on the face of the earth has three supply and demand variables:

1) Quality
2) Quantity
3) Price

All three elements apply to both the seller (the union) and the buyer (the city). Each entity can control only two of the elements. Based on these two controlled elements, the marketplace determines the third. If the city wants to determine the price and the quantity, it will have to accept the quality of applicants that the marketplace will yield. If the city wants to set the standards for quality and quantity, it will then have to pay the price demanded by the market. If the city is currently getting its desired quality and quantity, their needs are being met and there is no reason for them to pay more. Most cities believe their needs are being met. Your objective is to create dissatisfaction with the status quo.

The problem is identified by the first four research reports from Stage One:

1) Turnover Report
2) Staffing Report
3) Recruitment Report
4) Exit Interviews Report

Even if recruitment and retention are not currently a problem, they will be if the city does not maintain its competitive position in the market. Today's market leader that does not move above the current status quo soon becomes the last place loser. The argument is structured around either maintaining the current market position or improving upon it. The purpose of negotiations is selling something better than the current market position or at least not losing ground to the market. It is a constant process of selling up. If you haven't received a raise, even the current situation is worse than it was a year earlier. The market has moved up during the year. Standing still is losing ground to the market. If recruitment and retention numbers are currently acceptable, use these arguments:

"In order to continue our ability to recruit and retain the best employees, we cannot lose our competitive edge. One thing we can be certain about is that the market will move away from us if we become complacent. Other departments are envious of our recruits. They are constantly working to attract our applicants and new hires. Let's make sure that does not happen."

"We need to raise our hiring standards. As a result, we will be drawing from a smaller applicant pool and we will be in competition with Gotham City."

The department does not have to be in a state of despair for there to be a problem. Even Tiger Woods has a problem – younger "Tigers" breathing down his neck. If he hopes to remain on top, he will have to continually strive to do more and to do it better.

Step Two - The Cause

There is just one cause – a compensation and benefits package that is not competitive. Period. How do we know this? The exit interviews and the wage survey tell us so. At this point, do not be concerned about the components of wages and benefits, but the aggregate value of the total compensation package.

Step Three - The Solution

There is only one solution – a more competitive compensation and benefits package.

This is very important to remember – the argument must be presented and articulated up front. This means before any proposals are submitted or any political activities are attempted, the argument must be fully articulated. No argument? Then there is nothing to talk about. Begin developing the argument as soon as the research is completed. The argument is essential to everything done from this point forward. The argument must be articulated to the appropriate recipients to be of any value.

Step Four - The Message

The message is a single sentence that fully states the argument:

> *"Currently, we are not able to attract and retain a sufficient number of qualified officers because we are not competitive with other cities in our market."*

The solution is not explicitly stated. The listener will easily infer the proper solution. This is more effective than stating it directly. The message must always be in the form of pretext, not your ultimate objective. What this means, is that your message should be a statement that presents an argument that addresses an issue other than your real objective, but that will help you obtain that objective.

Step Five - The Talking Points

Talking points provide evidence that supports the message:

1) The number of applicants has declined in recent years
2) More than one-half of the new hires leave before 5 years of service
3) The compensation package is below the market average
4) The department has the lowest requirements for applicants

Talking points must be in the form of subtext, not the actual solution. This means you will provide evidence or solutions that address a problem other than the one you want rectified, but that will also solve your problem.

Step Six - The Stump Speech

The Stump Speech is a short (15 minute) talk that can be compressed or expanded depending on the time requirements for a certain venue. It has to be concise and to the point. The stump speech is a compilation of the message and the talking points. You must have it in writing, not just an outline. It must be rehearsed over and over. The presenter must be able to deliver it each and every time with the same enthusiasm as the first delivery. Never deviate from the prepared text. Probable questions that may be asked by your audience after the presentation must be identified. Concise and to the point answers must then be prepared in advance. If someone throws a curve ball, just deflect it.

"That's a good question. Here's what has been happening ... "

Then go straight into the standard, prepared answers. The purpose of the stump speech is to deliver the message and reinforce it with the talking points. It is not to provide group therapy for the audience. No matter how trite and repetitious the speech may sound, it has to be given over and over – every time there is an opportunity.

A good stump speech has six elements:

1) Develop rapport with the audience
2) Tell the problem (pretext)
3) Tell the cause (pretext)
4) Suggest the solution (subtext)
5) Create a sense of urgency (subtext)
6) Tell the audience what they can do (subtext)

CHAPTER 3

Stage Three:
Establish Key Relationships

Effective relationships must be developed with the key players who will determine the outcome of contract negotiations. Contact must be made with each person in the proper order as to not offend one of the others on the list. This must be done before any public relations campaign. There are three major groups that have the most influence:

1) The inside power brokers
2) The inside bureaucrats
3) The outside power brokers

Step One - The Inside Power Brokers

In this step, we will discuss what I refer to as the inside power brokers. These are the first people you will need to deal with when establishing your new relationships. The inside power brokers are all included as a single step because each relationship developed among this group of people is related to the others. If you aren't careful, your relationship with one of these people could destroy your relationship with another. For this reason, it is very important that when you are dealing with one of these inside power brokers you consider how your actions will be seen by the others in this group and what consequences you may face. There are three inside power brokers:

1) The Police Chief
2) The Mayor or City Administrator
3) The City Council

The Police Chief

All of the inside power brokers exert significant influence on virtually every decision concerning the police department. The police chief has direct control of the department's day-to-day operations. The other two inside power brokers see him as their resident authority on how a police department should be ran. While the chief has limited power concerning the size of the department's budget, he alone makes virtually all of the other decisions. He even has veto power over expenditures. If he is opposed to some type of expenditure, the mayor and the council will generally go along with his judgment.

To succeed, it will be necessary to have a good working relationship with the chief. Most union leaders think that getting along with the chief is a sign of weakness on their part. It is true that a large portion of the union membership wants a union president that is in a constant state of war with the chief. It may feel good seeing the president mugging the chief, but in the end it costs the police officers plenty. Most police unions hate the chief and see him as the focus of all that is wrong with the department. The chief is seen as an incompetent fool occupying a position of power that is hell bent on abusing officers and destroying the department while grabbing all the fanfare he can to satisfy his inflated ego. If only they could get the chief fired, everything would be better. Even if they could get rid of the chief, the members will soon hate the new chief.

I'm not saying that the union should go along with everything the chief says just to get on his good side. There should be conflict with the chief at times. The goals of the department and the union membership are not always the same. When these situations occur, it should be handled by someone other than the union president. All of the efforts to build a relationship between the chief and the union president can be thwarted by one grievance. Do not let the union president handle grievances. The person handling grievances should be far removed from political activities and the negotiations process.

To build a proper relationship, the union must avoid conflicts with the chief and never have a vote of no confidence – NEVER! It is not your place to decide whether the chief goes or stays. In our market economy, the boss selects the employees, the employees do not select the boss. The police department is a monarchy, not a democracy. Every successful organization that provides goods or services in our society is organized as a monarchy. Democracy is great for writing the rules of society but horrible for producing goods and services.

A smart union president will have weekly meetings with the chief. With few exceptions, every desired change, including pay, should begin with the chief. He may not have the authority to make the decision on every issue, but his support or opposition will carry a lot of weight with the ultimate decision maker. Many times, union presidents claim that "the mayor thinks the chief is a baboon." If the mayor really believed that he would replace the chief. Most of the thoughts that police unions have about the chief are locker room fantasies. Either a way is found to deal with the man or you accept the consequences of him working against you during contract negotiations. This is the easiest relationship to cultivate. All of the others are more difficult. A strong chief can do much more for the union than a weak one.

The Mayor

There are two basic forms of local government in the United States. One is where the chief executive officer is elected by the public and is usually called the mayor. The other is where the mayor is actually the chairman of the city council and he has no executive authority. The council then hires an administrator to run the city. The terms mayor and administrator will be used interchangeably throughout this text.

The mayor controls all expenditures. The council may appropriate the money in the budget, but it is he who decides if the expenditures are actually made. The council may have the ability to tax but the mayor has the checkbook. In addition, the mayor has indirect control over every decision made in the police department. This is because he has the power to replace the chief. Don't think that the chief is not constantly aware of this. The police department is the chief's dukedom, but the mayor is the king. Effectively, the mayor can vicariously run the police department. Fortunately, few actually do. They have so many other responsibilities that being the de facto police commissioner is impractical.

A good police chief understands all of this and does not engage in reverse delegation with the mayor. The mayor influences the police department by telegraphing signals to the chief. If the chief is very smart, he knows how to translate these signals and act accordingly. His longevity is determined by this ability. Not correctly reading the signals and pushing decisions up to the mayor will normally cause the chief to become the ex-chief. The mayor is highly dependent on the chief.

The union president needs a good relationship with the mayor. There is just one major problem. The closer he appears to be with the mayor, the more his relationship with the chief erodes. If the chief thinks that you are too cozy with the mayor he will feel threatened and react in ways to bolster his authority. Suddenly, the influence with the chief is in jeopardy. What should your relationship be with the mayor? Well, you should not go fishing or golfing with him or invite him over for a cookout. Your relationship should be somewhat formal. In the event that you already have some personal relationship with the mayor, such as attending the same church, separate the relationships. While it is tempting to capitalize on that existing relationship, it can suddenly turn into a total mess. All you need from the mayor is his ear. You only need a relationship where the mayor trusts you and will be willing to sincerely read or listen to what you have to say. Having his ear is more important than anything that you might have to say. The most brilliant message that is never heard is of no consequence.

The City Council

Depending on who runs the city, the mayor or a hired administrator, the council's influence can be anywhere from weak to tyrannical. Under the mayoral system the council is usually weak. The council has no ability to remove the mayor, while the mayor has considerable power. Normally, he explains the rules to each councilman, one-by-one. It goes something like this:

> *"I'm the mayor. Only the electorate can fire me. While you and your fellow councilmen can appropriate money, it is I who controls whether the funds are actually expended. And, to a great degree, I can dictate where and how the funds are spent. You and I both want the same thing – whatever is best for our city. Here is how things will be handled. I will seek the council's input on major issues. Based on what I believe and the input from the council, I will attempt to make the correct decision. If we all cooperate, things will go very smoothly. However, if you try to buck me, I will make you and your constituents miserable. No streets will be repaired in your ward. I will reduce the number of police officers patrolling your ward. Parks in your ward will not be maintained. When I get through, your constituents will be circulating a recall petition on you. You can choose to do things the easy way or the hard way."*

Under this scenario, the council is usually powerless when it comes to influencing the mayor. The only people on the council that you want to approach are those who have a close relationship with him. It is not hard to find out who the mayor consistently listens to. However, beware of going too far. If the mayor thinks you are trying to use councilmen against him, you will receive the same wrath that the council fears. The mayor will be the one deciding whether you receive a pay increase, not the council. Focus on the mayor, but do not alienate the chief.

If your city has a hired administrator, then it is whole different ball game. Under this arrangement, the administrator is beholden to the council. He's not a toothless tiger, but he is required to closely follow the dictates of the council. With these circumstances, the council is very important. Get the council on your side and the administrator will normally go along, but beware of going around the administrator. If he thinks that you are trying to use the council to cram something down his throat, he may react in a manner that is not even in his best interest. Getting fired may be a major upheaval for you, but to a paid administrator it is just part of the job. Most administrators would rather be canned than have a group of subordinates pull a fast one on them.

Your relationship with the paid administrator should be similar to that of an elected mayor executive, but it should be even more businesslike. The mayor is probably a long-term resident and will have political influence after leaving office. Besides, your relationship with him, in one form or another, will last for life. The hired administrator is normally an outsider who has very little personal history with your city and will probably leave once he is no longer employed by the city. Actually, the hired administrator, who could be fired at the next council meeting, is better to deal with than the elected administrator who has job security that is not dependent on the city council.

Step Two – The Bureaucrats

There are three inside bureaucrats:

1) The City Attorney
2) The Finance Director
3) The Human Resources Director

One thing these three people have in common is that they cannot, or will not, help you. They can only harm you. They have a totally different agenda than the power brokers. They each see things through a narrow prism that only reflects things in a manner that they can relate to. If city hall should burn to the ground tonight, the city attorney would see the disaster as a legal problem – what liability might we incur? The finance director would see it as a money problem – what's this going to cost? The human resources director would see it as an employee problem – what are we going to do with the idle employees?

On the other hand, the mayor and the city council would have a more global view – how will we keep the city functioning? Oh, they also consider the bureaucrat's issues, but not as their primary concern. They see it as one small portion of the problem. If you try talking globally with the bureaucrats, you may as well be speaking Mandarin. They do not think globally. Each sees their field of expertise as their personal turf. They are primarily interested in defending their turf.

Although it may sound like I see the three bureaucrats as faceless robots, I do not. Each of these three is just a human being like everyone else and has to be treated accordingly – with dignity and respect. It is easy to demonize these people to fit our own perceptions – don't! However, I see these three as blockers – another impersonal label. I use this only as a descriptive term. The three combined see themselves as the city's goal-line defense. They believe that by defending their turf, they can trip you up and keep you from scoring. Most do this job very well.

Your relationship with the bureaucrats should be cordial, but one-sided – one-sided in their favor. You need to talk about their interests and issues, not yours. Developing a relationship with the bureaucrats has two purposes. One is to keep them from demonizing you. Once you get to know a person, it is hard to see that person as an evil caricature. The second, is to weaken their resolve to defeat you. You can forget about winning them over to your side. That will never happen, but you can mitigate their enthusiasm for seeking your demise.

Ego plays a very big part in the relationship with the bureaucrats, especially the attorney. Threaten a person's ego and all the progress you have made to-date is suddenly erased. Forget about your ego. They do not want to hear what you think concerning their area of expertise. Your purpose should be to seek their advice; not to give them advice about topics on which they are authorities and you are an amateur.

Step Three – The Outside Power Brokers

There may be many outside power brokers in your city, but there are two that you and all other police unions have. They are forces that must be dealt with. The two main outsiders are:

1) The Chamber of Commerce
2) The Local Press

There may be some others with similar influence, but normally these two are the heavyweights. I see these two as bomb throwers. They have no vote and they are not in the chain of command, but they can make or break the deal. The chamber and the press are estranged coconspirators. They are codependent. The chamber is composed primarily of conservative, republican, business people. They are big supporters of the police department, but they detest collective bargaining. Journalists are mostly liberal, democratic, idealists. They see the police department as heavy handed enforcers of property rights and the lower end of society as the victim of this enforcement.

Then why would I think they were coconspirators? What provides revenue for the media? It is ad sales, not the measly fifty cents you paid for a copy. Who buys the ads? Business people – the ones down at the chamber. This presents a rather strange marriage. One shows up at the church driving a Volkswagen Minibus and the other zooms in driving a BMW. So how does this diverse couple reconcile their competing points of view? Keep in mind, when given a choice, most people would prefer to attack their enemies rather than help their friends. And heaven forbid if you should provide aide and comfort to my enemy. They have a mutual understanding that each will attack their individual enemy while providing little for their friends.

The chamber sees the police department as their good friend, but finds the police union, that bulwark of socialism, to be public enemy number one. So as part of their agreement, the chamber ravages the police union, but only shows token support for the police department. The press sees the downtrodden as needing their support and blames the police department for the dismal state of affairs for the downtrodden. To maintain their side of the agreement, the press constantly attacks the police department and says very little about their concern for the "Great Class Struggle" – collective bargaining.

Unless you have been asleep, it should be apparent that they get you both coming and going. The chamber attacks your union and the press attacks your department.

The Chamber of Commerce

Many of you despise the chamber. Just as they see you as socialists, you see them as economic Nazis. Actually, these guys are a piece of cake. All you have to do is take their focus off of your union and put it on the police department. How do you do that? The first thing is for your union to join the chamber and become an active member. I might add, you need to be a positive and joyful member. The last thing you want to look like is the atheist who went to Sunday school. Do not go down there speaking that labor movement diatribe. Do not wear your union paraphernalia or your uniform either. If you do, you will be seen as a union thug and immediately disregarded.

The chamber is not going to provide much open support, but you can weaken their resolve to attack your union. There are only two options for the chamber – be your enemy or stay out of the fight. You want to keep them out of the fight.

The Local Press

Your goal with the press is to rehabilitate their opinion of the police department. You do this by providing information that they turn into news (the stuff that fits in around the advertisements or what they say in between car commercials). What kind of information can you provide to the press? You can give them anything that is in the public domain. If a citizen can obtain the information without violating the law, it is fair game. Why would the press need you if they can obtain it themselves? First, one has to know that it exists. It takes time to obtain the information. It usually requires some expertise to make sense of the data. And lastly, it takes someone who knows what he is doing to put the raw data into a report that the average newspaper reader can comprehend. For example, the Bureau of Justice Statistics releases a report on the changes in crime for the nation and local municipalities. You could take that data and prepare a report that compares your city to the national numbers and other comparable cities in your area. To do this, you could write a narrative explanation. Once written, give it to the press. Better yet, let the police chief give it to them. The local press is starving for local news that is relevant to their audience. Most days, the press is scraping the barrel for local news.

The press is not going to provide much open support, but you can weaken their resolve to attack your department. There are only two options for the press – be your enemy or stay out of the fight. You want to keep them out of the fight.

CHAPTER 4

Stage Four:
Generate Public Support

Most of you are wondering how much this is going to cost. I am
here to tell you that it will not cost a single penny. It might even
save you money. Notice, I am talking about money. There is a cost,
but it comes in the form of time and effort. How are you going to get
newspaper ads, television spots, and billboards without spending
any money? It is simple. You don't need or want those things. They
don't work. Remember, when I told you earlier that you needed to
create a stump speech? I didn't say a Madison Avenue television
spot. Do you know why it is called a stump speech? It is because
real politicians once went from town to town to give their speech.
They would use anything to elevate them above the crowd. Many
times, it was a tree stump. To succeed with a local issue on a local
level you do not need the mass media to disseminate your message.
You simply need to go on the rubber chicken circuit. Attend a few

civic club meetings and you will understand why it is called the rubber chicken circuit.

I teased you with the proposition that you can actually save money. Here's how that works. You get rid of all of your negative campaign activities, including:

1) Billboard signs calling the mayor a bum
2) Banner planes calling the chief a jerk
3) Throwing money at political candidates
4) Newspaper ads that show you complaining and begging

Unless you have a death wish, you should get rid of your PAC and your fund solicitations. You can either behave like an astute political operative or you can prostitute yourself by extorting money from the public to support your political bribery. Telephone solicitations are nothing but legalized extortion. Political contributions by people with a direct, vested interest (attached to a quid pro quo) are nothing short of bribery. Most of these activities backfire (the politician either does not deliver or gets defeated). The typical police PAC is about as savvy and effective as The Three Stooges. Giving money to politicians is like buying sex. It has little lasting effect. Learn the art of seduction and you can go much further.

Step One –The Rubber Chicken Circuit

Press your suit, master your stump speech and head out on the rubber chicken circuit. First stop? The good ole boys' club! Virginia Slims said, "you've come a long way baby," but I'm here to tell you the good ole boys' club is alive and well today. All of the Gloria Steinem's and Betty Freidan's have not been able to bring it down. Oh, they have let a few women in, and as unfair as it might be, the boys still have the votes. And just where does this bastion of machismo hold court? It resides in rather benign sounding places:

1) The Chamber of Commerce
2) The Rotary Club
3) The Kiwanis Club
4) The Lions Club
5) The Optimists Club

There are many other similar organizations that could be added to this list, but this should give you some idea of what I am talking about. This combined group of organizations wields a lot of influence in most cities in the United States. The best way to get your message to these people is for you and your executive board to be members – good members, working for the good of the community. However, you will get the broadest coverage by giving your stump speech to each organization. These groups are constantly seeking luncheon speakers. It is hard to line up a new speaker each week. The Chamber of Commerce and other similar business and economic groups allow the press to attend their events and report on what was said by the guest speakers. The civic clubs usually do not allow this.

Step Two – Dealing with Opinion Leaders

Opinion leaders are people who are looked to for political direction in their local neighborhoods. This is normally found in minority neighborhoods, primarily Black and Hispanic neighborhoods. If your city is 30 percent Black and 20 percent Hispanic, you will need the support of these communities. For the most part, you are not going to reach them on the rubber chicken circuit.

In the Black community, which is predominately Baptist, the opinion leaders are often the local ministers. Keep in mind, the ones that matter are the ones that have a church and preach there every Sunday, not the hustlers who are only running shakedowns on businesses. Most cities have a local Black ministerial alliance. Building a relationship with this group can be very beneficial. They want their neighborhoods to be safe, just as you do. They are willing to work with you to accomplish that goal. Maybe you are Black and think that you get a bye on this. Wrong! When you put on that uniform, you are no longer seen as a "brother." You are then seen as "the man." Go and cultivate those relationships. It will help your union, the community, your department, and your city.

The Hispanic community, which is predominantly Catholic, has political figures sometimes referred to as Caudillos, who are looked up to when it comes to political matters. You need to identify and deal with these people one-on-one. Also, the Padre at the local parish has a lot of influence. Whether he will exercise that influence is another matter, but it is a good idea to be on speaking terms with him. Again, he wants the same thing you want for his community.

Who should deliver the message to these people? The chief – the same guy you have vowed to destroy. The chief will be better accepted, more likely to be heard, and have more impact than the most silver throated member of your union. If the chief is incapable or unwilling to perform this function, the responsibility falls to the union president. For this reason, the union president must stay out of the day-to-day battles between the city and the union. Someone else needs to be doing the dirty work of fighting.

CHAPTER 5

Stage Five:
Plan Your Strategy

This is the point where you begin to develop the game plan for negotiations. Forget all of the dumb stuff that is widely taught and used across the country. The word strategy implies that you use your brain. The strategy I am talking about demands it. Let's go through the following steps one at a time:

1) Separate the issues
2) Determine the decision process
3) The monetary issues
4) The non-monetary issues
5) The pre-negotiations agenda
6) Establish benchmarks and timetable
7) Determine strike zone
8) Select negotiating team
9) Set expectations

Step One – Separate the Issues

You probably think there are an unlimited number of issues that could be raised during negotiations. There aren't. There are only two:

1) More money
2) More restrictions on the chief

More Money

Anything that costs money is more money, such as:

1) Increase in the pay matrix
2) Higher clothing allowance
3) Increase in insurance contribution by the city
4) More paid time off

The list goes on and on. Many people think that more paid time off is a freebie. It is not. To maintain the current on-duty strength, more officers will have to be hired.

More Restrictions on the Chief

Anything that takes decision-making power away from the chief is a restriction on the chief. Here are some examples:

1) Grievance procedures
2) Promotion procedures
3) Discipline procedures
4) Shift and vacation bidding

Again, the list could go on and on. All of these procedures strip the chief of the authority to unilaterally make decisions. Many of these restrictions are desired by the chief. I do not know of a chief who wants to arbitrarily make vacation assignments. While these procedures restrict the chief, they also provide cover for him. He does not have to take the heat that comes from firings and suspensions or even promotions.

Step Two – Determine the Decision Process

The decision processes for more money and more restrictions are not the same. The administrator and the council are only concerned with the money. They could care less about the internal workings of the police department. The chief, on the other hand, is very concerned about the way the operations of the department are handled. It can mean the difference between success and failure for him and his command staff. To complicate matters, there is usually someone on the command staff that is organizing a stealthy insurrection against the chief. This is in addition to the union trying to weaken his authority. The chief is constantly under attack from all sides. On monetary items, the chief has little input. Monetary and operational issues must be separated.

Step Three – The Monetary Issues

The first step in diagramming the decision process for any potential issue is to identify the ultimate decision maker. If the administrator is an elected official, such as the mayor, he is your guy. Even if the administrator is a hired professional, he will probably be the decision maker. However, it could be someone on the council. It could be someone with no official connection to city hall, such as a judge or local state legislator. And heaven forbid, legal man (the city attorney) may have everyone cowed down and he is calling the shots. I have seen that. Whoever it is, we need to know. The second step is to determine how the question gets to the decision maker. There is a path that the information follows.

To the uninformed, the process looks rather obvious. It is not. Theoretically, the administrator crafts a proposal based on his research or a suggestion from someone on the council. He submits his proposal to the head of the city council, who then sends it to the appropriate committees for review. The committees hold hearings and then give their recommendations to the council as a whole. The council then debates the recommendations and votes to accept, amend, or reject the recommendations. Finally, the administrator implements the actions voted on by the council.

In reality, the decision process begins and ends with the ultimate decision maker – the mayor. If the decision maker opposes the idea up front, it is D.O.A. If the decision maker is not opposed to the idea, the issue has a chance, as long as it can endure the torturous obstacle course. Think of the process like the Indy 500. The administrator is the flagman who starts the race and waves the checkered flag at the winner – 250 grueling laps later. He can black flag you and you are out of the race. How does the administrator decide what to support and what to pan? He asks himself five questions:

1) Is this a good idea based on my values?
2) Is there broad support for the issue?
3) How much political capital will I have to spend?
4) What is the potential reward for me?
5) What is the potential risk for me?

If the idea scores favorably, he puts the full court press into action. If the score is low, he lets it twist in the wind. If the score is in the middle, he will not kill the idea, but he will let the sponsor fight a guerilla war throughout the process while providing little help. If the issue survives the process, he will approve it, providing that the sponsor gives him a political chip.

One thing that you must keep in mind is that you will be dealing with just one portion of city government – the police department. With few exceptions, the decision maker's expert and consultant on the police department is the police chief. It should be obvious that having the chief on board right up front is a good idea. While we want to begin the process with the administrator, we want to be absolutely certain that his consultant (the chief) is not going to give the idea the thumbs down.

So where do we begin with the decision maker? We help him answer the five basic questions. If you are unable to satisfactorily address each question, then you are finished. You might as well go back to the union hall and have a beer. The questions may be the property of the decision maker, but the appropriate answers are your responsibility. Unless you can deliver answers that meet his criteria, you are blown up. Let's go through each question one at a time.

Is this a good idea, based on my values?

I can tell you straight up that a pay raise is not a good idea. It is always a bad idea. You must follow the argument trail that presents the problem (his problem) followed by the cause and the solution. The solution is a pay raise, but that can never be the issue. Improving recruitment and retention are good ideas. Improving the caliber of people in the department is a good idea. Remember this – better department good, pay raise bad. Forget about the pay raise and concentrate on the real problems – recruitment and retention. Solving these problems leads to the money.

Is there broad support for the issue?

Do you really expect the decision maker to carry the ball for you if there is little support for the idea? How much support does your department have from your community for improving the department? Come on, tell the truth. There is squat. Whose fault is that? It's yours. Go in the men's room and look in the mirror. Staring you straight in the face is public enemy number one when it comes to garnering support for the police department. I bet you cannot tell me the number of true supporters you have on the council. I will go even further; you cannot tell me the name of every person on the council without looking at a list. Oh, change must be coming – big change.

How much political capital will I have to spend?

For the decision maker to go to the mat and expend a lot of his political capital, he will have to have a major investment in the idea, both personally and politically. Few issues rise to this level. How much capital would he use to get you a pay raise? Zero! How much capital would he spend to deal with a recruitment and retention problem? Not much, unless "Take This Job and Shove It" has become the anthem at the police station. I know what you are thinking, why are we wasting all of our effort on promoting recruitment and retention? You are focused on the wrong thing. We do not want to persuade this guy to burn a large amount of his political favors to get our issue passed. We must be concerned with reducing the number of chips he will have to spend. The best case scenario has him spending nothing. If you are having a problem understanding this, go back to the last question.

What is the potential reward for me?

Ah, the reward. Everyone loves the reward. The taste of success is never too sweet. What possible reward could there be for the decision maker to support our issue? There is only one – taking credit for identifying a problem and providing the correct solution. He has "fixed" a problem in the police department; ergo he has made our city a better place. There has to be a quid pro quo in place – he helps you, he gets all the glory if the project is a success.

What is the potential risk for me?

Success may be heaven, but failure is hell. The risk he abhors is the blame that comes with failure. Issues at the political level are not controlled tests done in a sterile laboratory. They are personal. They consume the ego and pride of the standard bearers. The bitter vetch of failure is what we all try to avoid. In this scenario, the pro quo is he helps you, you take the responsibility and blame if the project is a failure.

If your issue survives the process, the decision maker gets the glory, you get the money. If your issue is assassinated at some point in the process, you take a fall and the decision maker escapes with his ego and reputation in tact. You live to fight the good fight again.

Step Four – The Non-Monetary Issues

"Mr. Police Chief, sir? Would you kindly don this straight jacket and allow me to put these leg irons on you? If you will, it will make me and my fellow officers so very happy. You see, we think that you are an incompetent nincompoop who cannot exercise proper judgment."

Laugh if you want, but this is the message that the chief hears when you propose restrictions on his authority. Let me ask you this; is your chief going along with the straight jacket and the leg irons? Probably not. So what do you do? I bet you take these types of issues to the negotiating table and try to get the city to cram them down the chief's throat. Are you having any success? Again, probably not. The reason you are not is because the city is not interested in these issues. After you present them at the negotiating table, the city's negotiator tells the administrator, who then calls his resident expert on the police department. You guessed it, it's the chief. You can figure out the rest.

All of the non-monetary issues must be discussed with the chief as they arise, not just at contract time. Use side letters to memorialize any agreements. You can then have them added to the contract at the next negotiating cycle. Since the chief has already bought in, adding them to the contract is just a ministerial function.

What if you cannot come to an agreement with the chief? Then you better come up with a different angle to address the issue. The odds of the administrator forcing these types of changes on the chief are virtually nil. If he does, you can start planning for the chief's retirement party. As for getting an arbitrator to impose the change, don't be too optimistic. If the evidence is so pervasive that you could convince an arbitrator, you should be able to come to a deal with the chief.

How do you deal with the chief? First, you should deal with problems when they arise. The sooner you deal with them, the better the chance of getting a successful resolution. Unlike the methodology used for monetary issues, you want to state the problem from your perspective. Within the close confines of the police department, anything that is a problem for you eventually becomes a problem for the chief. Go to the chief and say:

"Chief, we have this problem. How can we make it go away?"

There is no need for assigning blame, just identify the problem. Together, you and the chief identify the cause and then try to craft a solution that is satisfactory to both of you. Be open-minded. Keep in mind that most problems are the result of you having a jackass among your rank and file officers and the chief having a jackass in a supervisory position. Most schisms involve repeat offenders. Don't expect the chief to give up his guy any sooner than you are willing to offer up your guy. Besides, burnt offerings accomplish nothing.

Step Five – The Pre-Negotiations Agenda

For the typical agenda:

1) Obtain chief's blessing
2) Float issue by the administrator
3) Work on bureaucrats
4) Begin public relations program
5) Ask for administrator's support
6) Begin lobbying council
7) Ramp up public relations program
8) Seek commitment from individual councilmen

Obtain Chief's Blessing

If you cannot get the chief's blessing for improving recruitment and retention, you may as well resign your position in the union and let someone else do the job. Actually, we want more from the chief than his blessing. We want him leading the charge. The chief is the one person who can give the best presentation of the message. To most citizens, he is the personification of the police department.

Float Issue by the Administrator

The administrator has to be aware that there is a problem and that the police department is working to identify the cause and possible solutions. You cannot be out talking to the community about the problem before the administrator has been briefed. If the first wind of the issue reaches the administrator by way of the grapevine, you are probably doomed. Who should brief the administrator? The chief! If the chief cannot or will not do it, then you must.

Work on Bureaucrats

Legal guy, finance guy, and H.R. guy must be dealt with early in the process. Once they have developed their lethal weapon to destroy your plan, it is too late. Not only will they make a direct frontal assault on your issue, they will try to erode any support from the administrator. This triad of negativity can have your caravan in the ditch before you can get up to full speed. Don't hesitate. Get to them before they stop you.

Begin Public Relations Program

Public relations are how you take your message to the public at large. By now, you have a message, talking points, and a stump speech. They must be disseminated to be of any real value. They are of no consequence if they are buried in your portfolio.

Ask for Administrator's Support

Before you ask the administrator to buy into your issue, you must demonstrate that there is support for it. If your public relations program is gaining traction, he will notice. Do not be discouraged if he takes a wait-and-see approach. Once he tells you that he is reserving his decision, you have the green light to put the pedal to the metal on public relations. If you go full-bore prior to seeking his support, he may see it as you trying to apply pressure on him. Remember, you only have to ask for his support.

Begin Lobbying City Council

Even if your city council is powerless, you do not want to offend them. If you are promoting your issue like a traveling evangelist and you have not discussed it with individual councilmen, they will think that you have no respect for them. In the event that they actually call the shots, avoiding them could be fatal to your plans.

Ramp up Public Relations Program

Once all of the principal players have been tactfully dealt with, your public relations program can be put into high gear without fear of having someone feel like they have been snubbed.

Seek Commitment from Individual Councilmen

We are nearing the end of the process. Our goal at this point is not to turn the councilmen into cheerleaders, but to make sure that none of them throw a shoe and jump over the fence. One single councilman going out on some crazy tangent could destroy all of the work that has been done. Provide them comfort and solace. We do not need to convert them to police groupies. We just want to make sure that they do not get mad at us.

Step Six – Establish Benchmarks and Timetable

Prior to actually beginning negotiations, you must answer three essential questions. Without these answers you will be lost from the start. These questions are:

1) What is your goal?
2) When will you walk away from the table?
3) What are you going to do when you walk away from the table?

What is your goal?

You probably think that your goal should be some fixed amount – it should not. Your goal should always be:

"A plan to get our department to the proper place in the market."

That's it. Obviously, there have to be numbers attached to it at some point, but your goal should be totally flexible in the beginning. If you are considerably behind the market, it may take more than one contract cycle to achieve your goal. How that goal is achieved should also be open for discussion. Simply seeking changes in the pay matrix may doom you to defeat. Most cities try to force the same deal on all of their bargaining units under the banner, using "pattern bargaining" or parity. Unless you are willing to negotiate for all of the other unions, you will need to be both flexible and creative.

When will you walk away from the table?

Why would you want to walk away from the table? You do this if you think that your options away from the table are better than dealing with the city's negotiating team. Most successful negotiations will require that you walk away from the table at some point. You can always come back, no explanation required. The typical city does not get serious until this happens. Declaring impasse is normally translated as, "Oh, you really want to negotiate?" Walking away from the table does not require any theatrics or emotions. The best way to walk away is to just not return. You do have to tell the city that you do not want to negotiate any longer.

So, when should you walk away? The first criteria would be time. If you have been negotiating for several months (notice I said months, not years) and the end is nowhere in sight, it is probably time to walk. The second criteria would be dollar oriented. If it appears that the city is unwilling or unable to move any higher and they are not in the relevant range (at or above the least you will accept) then it's time to go.

What are you going to do when you walk away from the table?

This is very important. You must have a "Plan B" or you are toast. If you have no "Plan B," walking away from the table will accomplish nothing. If you don't have one, get one. Here are some possibilities:

1) Mediation
2) Fact Finding
3) Arbitration
4) Go around the negotiator and deal with the mayor directly
5) Go to the council directly

6) Take it to the street (not a job action)
7) Take whatever the city is offering

Whatever you do, it has to be something the city's team does not
want you to do, unless you take whatever they are offering. One
thing to keep in mind is that to be effective, you have to just walk
away. If you start negotiations by threatening to go to "Plan B"
and constantly bring it up every time you are unhappy with city's
negotiators, they will become inoculated against this tactic and
when you actually make good on your threat it will have little
impact.

Okay, you understand the goal, but how do you determine a walk
away amount? Let us assume that your department is currently 6
percent below the market average and you believe the average is
where you belong. If you are going to be negotiating a three year
contract setting your bottom line at 2 percent per year would be
simple-minded (forget about compounding for now). Three raises
of 2 percent would only get you to the market if all of the other
departments in the market took three zeroes. The chances of that
happening are slim. Based on current economic conditions, the
other departments will receive from 3 ½ percent to 4 percent per
year. For you to get to the market average, you will have to get
the three 2 percent raises plus whatever the market receives. It is
rather apparent that setting 2 percent each year as the bottom line
would be foolish.

What if the city has you over a barrel and is beating the hell out of
you, claiming poverty and other terrible consequences if they try
to close the gap between your department and the market? I am
betting you would not accept any proposal that would result in you
falling further behind the market. If that is the case, your bottom

line is somewhere between 3 ½ percent to 4 percent. This is just an illustration, but this is the process you should follow to identify your bottom line.

Now that you have answered your three questions, you have to repeat the process for the city. This will be more difficult because while you know what is going on in your mind, you can only guess what they are thinking. People ask me all the time, "How are we supposed to determine what they are thinking?" My answer to you is to do it the same way you solve crimes. Enlist your detectives and Internal Affairs. Most cities have a "Plan C" – cram their offer down your throat. It happens all of the time.

Step Seven - Determine Strike Zone

Now that we know your bottom line and we have estimated the city's top line, we know the strike zone. If your bottom line is 4 percent per year and the city's top line is 5 percent per year, we know the range for a possible agreement would be between 4 percent and 5 percent per year. Sure, you would agree to 6 percent each year, but the city will walk before they agree to anything greater than 5 percent. The city would like to buy you out at 2 percent, but you will be heading for the exit before that ever happens. So, whether we like it or not, if we hope to make a deal with these guys, we will have to be willing to accept something between 4 percent and 5 percent per year.

Negotiations are much like baseball. You get three pitches outside of the strike zone and two pitches inside the strike zone. On ball four, the city walks. On strike three, you head for the dugout. This means that our first three pitches will be outside of the strike zone –

greater than 5 percent. From that point forward we will have to be inside the strike zone.

That now leads us to pitch selection. What should your first pitch be? How about a 100-mile per hour fastball high and outside? No, save the fast ball for the final strike. Your first pitch should be a breaking ball that is high and outside – 6 percent. I know, you are wondering how I settled on 6 percent. How wide is the strike zone? It is 1 percent. This is the amount that your first proposal should exceed the city's top line. If the strike zone had been 2 percent, we would have started at 2 percent above the city's top line. Most people think that your first proposal should be really high, hoping that you might get the city to settle for something greater than their 5 percent ceiling. It's not going to happen. Starting high and then making large or numerous counters that get you closer to reality only destroys your credibility. It is better to start with an amount that does not totally alienate the other side and then make only small concessions. This is not the Tijuana flea market where the seller asks $100 for a $2 item.

Step Eight – Select Negotiating Team

Many times, little thought goes into selecting the negotiating team. It usually consists of executive board members and a couple of rabid dogs. You do not want any of these people on the team. First of all, the team should be small. The larger the team, the less chance there is of reaching an agreement. The best negotiations occur when each negotiating team has only one person. The president of the union is more valuable off of the team than on it. The best negotiations also occur away from the table. The president should be leading the unofficial negotiations. Next, we have the mad dogs. Most members of the union think that these fire breathing beasts can intimidate the city and get the deal done. They cannot. They only screw up the process. Leave them off the team. Now comes the question of whether you should include your attorney. First of all, being an attorney is no qualification as a negotiator. If your attorney has both a brain and negotiating skills then he can be a valuable asset to the team. On the other hand, if he only wants to play "lawyerball" with the city's attorney and thinks that the rules and procedures of civil litigation apply to negotiations, then you need to bounce him. There is a time and a place for that lawyer crap, but it is not during your negotiations.

Step Nine – Set Expectations

Unless you set the expectations of your membership, you will eventually have a collision of unreasonable expectations and political reality. Expectations will quickly become unrealistic if they are not reigned in early on. What should be the appropriate expectations?

"A plan to get our department to the proper place in the market."

If you have some loud mouth demanding some outrageous increase in pay, ask how he would go about obtaining it. He will not have a clue. Ask if he has any inside information or special relationship with the decision makers. Again, he will not. Wanting and demanding something is totally different from getting it.

CHAPTER 6

Stage Six:
Negotiate the Deal

Most unions pin all of their hopes on "The Table." The table is
where most unions start the negotiating process. Everything we
have discussed prior to this has been ignored. They just arrive
at the table, at the appointed time, for the first session and begin
trying to cajole the city into buying some unreasonable proposal.
They have no idea what they will say; let alone what they should say.
Here is what you should do, step-by-step:

1) Negotiate the agenda
2) Tell them your goal
3) Tell them the impasse date
4) Tell them the problem
5) Tell them the cause
6) Show them what it will take to rectify the problem
7) Show them what a 1 percent raise will cost

8) Tackle the ability-to-pay issue
9) Make your initial proposal
10) Get the city's initial proposal
11) Make mutual concessions
12) Agree or declare impasse
13) Dump the formal negotiations
14) Go back to the formal negotiations
15) Deal with "Howard Hughes"
16) Get the deal ratified

Step One - Negotiate the Agenda

Everything begins with establishing an agenda. The agenda should be simple. It should only cover when, where, how long and how often you will meet. Actually, the agenda only needs to be negotiated one meeting at a time. What you do not want to agree to are restrictive ground rules. The most common is a gag rule. Remember the "Plan B" we discussed? Unless you have absolute and final binding arbitration as your "Plan B," you will be greatly harmed by a gag rule. For the most part, you do not want to be blabbing your mouth about what is said at the negotiating sessions. Running to the press with every detail is self defeating. However, if the city's negotiator is stonewalling you and not getting your message to the decision maker, you are screwed if you have agreed to their gag rule. No matter what the level of cooperation is, the union president needs to be talking with the decision makers throughout the negotiating cycle. I always hear from someone that doing that would be acting in bad faith and committing an unfair labor practice. Listen, if the mayor is talking to you and the mayor is the city attorney's boss, who is going to file this complaint? Even if legal man was stupid enough to do that, it would go nowhere. One thing cities have taught us is that unfair labor practice complaints aren't worth the paper they are filed on. They normally die of old age.

Step Two - Tell Them Your Goal

If you do not know the goal by now, pack your books and head to the principal's office. You have failed this course. There is one and only one goal. It makes no difference if you are the New York City PBA or the Bugtussle FOP, your goal is:

"A plan to get our department to the proper place in the market."

If you think this line is too simple and corny, then you need to resign from the negotiating team. You are about as worthless as a television evangelist who is ashamed to say "Jesus saves." If you are uncomfortable repeating the goal, over and over, you need to go. "A plan to get our department to the proper place in the market," should become your battle cry. If it is not repeated at least 1,000 times prior to and during negotiations, you are derelict in your duties. Come on man, you've got to believe.

Step Three - Tell Them the Impasse Date

Unless you tell them that there is a point where you will walk away based on the calendar, the city will negotiate with you into the next millennium. The city thinks that they are happy with the status quo – you have to convince them otherwise. If you drag negotiations on for several years after the expiration of the contract, the typical settlement involves no retroactive pay. This is a big savings for the city and a moral victory. Your head on a pole will be displayed to other unions in the city as a warning against playing "hardball" with them. Tell them the date.

Step Four - Tell Them the Problem

I know, they will have it memorized by now because you have
already told everyone in the city the problem. Keep talking about
the problem until they buy into it. There is no sense moving on
to the next step if they do not think that they have a problem. If
it appears that you are getting stuck on this issue, start trying to
determine why they think there is not a problem. You can share
some summaries of your research to back up what you say, but
do not give them the entire set of data. Odds are that you will get
nowhere with the city's negotiating team, because they do not have
the foggiest idea whether or not there is a problem. They have not
done any research; or, if they have, it is so amateurish that Mickey
Mouse would laugh at it.

So, what should you do? Remember how I told you that the union
president should not be on the negotiating team? Now is when
that becomes important. To get something done concerning the
problem, the city's negotiation team will need some direction. It
cannot come from the union. It has to come from the mayor. We
need the union president and the chief talking into the mayor's ear.
If your lawyer starts reciting that unfair labor practice baloney, fire
him. You need someone who is working with you to get a deal, not
some zealot who is worshipping legal positivism and the bar's so
called "ethics." These "ethics" are actually the lawyers' union work
rules.

You might understand the union president being inclined to
whisper into the mayor's ear, but the chief? You want the chief, a
contented chief, or one of his deputy chiefs at the negotiating table.
Just getting him there is often tough. Many chiefs remind me of a
little boy who is being forced to put on short pants, suspenders, and

a bow tie to wear to church. There is a whole lot of resistance. You need him there. How do you make him contented? Do not take the non-monetary items to the table for resolution. Settle all of them in advance, away from the table. The chief does not have to carry your case for you. He just needs to tell the truth. If you are in a constant state of war with him and you have ten "poison pill" non-monetary items at the table, the chief is going to behave like a terrorist.

To be an actionable problem, there has to be a sense of urgency attached to the problem that is perceived to be very important. The problem needs to be here and now, screaming for attention. The reason the Congress does not make major changes in Social Security is because there is no sense of urgency. The problem is seen as something far removed from the present. There are two major elements to any problem:

1) Importance
2) Urgency

People create their to-do lists in the following order:

1) High urgency – High importance
2) High urgency – Low importance
3) Low urgency – High importance
4) Low urgency – Low importance

You want recruitment and retention in the police department to be number one on the decision maker's list. To be successful, you will need to elevate the importance of the issue and create a sense of urgency.

Step Five – Tell Them the Cause

What is the cause? Right, a wage and benefits package that is not competitive. How do we know that? Because our wage survey tells us so, that's how. Give the city a chart that shows how your department compares with the other cities in your market survey. It should only show a percentage ranking. Do not give them anything else. If you give them your survey, the discussion will immediately turn into a debate about your survey. Even if they cannot find fault with your survey (they will), they will not believe your numbers. The purpose of your first exhibit is to let them know how you think you compare with the other departments. Just like with the previous step, do not move on until the city buys into the cause. They do not have to accept your numbers, only the basic concept that you are behind or you will soon be behind where you belong.

It is usually at this point that the city will try to deflect you by saying that all of this is superfluous because they do not have the money. In all likelihood, they are lying to you. If you have had the ability-to-pay study done, you will know if they are telling the truth or not. As tempting as it may be, do not challenge this claim. Sure you could tear them to shreds, but what would it accomplish? You would only alienate and anger them and still be faced with having to deal with them. Only now, they are irate and hell bent on taking you out. Control your anger and go for the jugular on the issue of inadequate compensation. Say this:

> *"So, what you are telling me is that you realize that our compensation package is not where it should be and you would support fixing it if you had the money, but you do not? Is that correct? Okay, I understand that. If you do not have the money, you do not have the money. As much as we do not like it, we hear you."*

Handle this correctly, and you have cleared the first hurdle – getting them to concede that the pay is too low. I know, they have just told you a whopper, but let's move on. We will deal with their mendacity later.

Step Six – Show Them What it Will Take to Rectify the Problem

As we have discussed earlier, a plan that gets your department to today's market price over a three year contract is a loser. The market will move away from its current position, leaving you to remain behind the market. At this point, present a matrix that shows what it would take to get you to the market based on various assumptions for the average move of the market. Just because the city has tried to preempt the discussion by claiming poverty does not mean that you should abandon your program. Do not go to the next step until the city's team fully understands the matrix.

Step Seven – Show Them What a One Percent Raise Will Cost

Again, they will tell you that you are wasting time because they cannot afford it no matter how much it costs. Ask them to indulge you. Even if the city cannot afford to increase the pay, we will all know what the amount that cannot be afforded is. Just as with the previous steps, do not move on until they have bought in.

Step Eight – Tackling the Ability-to-Pay Issue

If you have successfully reached this point, you can begin addressing the ability-to-pay hurdle. At this point you probably have two things that you are certain about:

1) The city is lying about their finances
2) You know that they are lying

You need to add one more thing:

3) They know you know that they are lying

This requires some finesse. Think of it like defusing an exploding device. If you are not delicate, you will be blown up. You do this by asking questions and feeding them small abstracts of their audited financial statements. Be careful not to ask so many questions that they bring in the finance director with his apocalyptic PowerPoint presentation. Every finance director on the face of the earth has one of those doom and gloom slide shows. There is nothing you can do about that. It is just the bean counter mentality. If, however, you get sucked into listening to this prophecy by the grim reaper, just sit back and listen. Do not ask questions or try to argue with him. It's a waste of time. Once he has left, just pretend that he was never there.

This is a point where you will have to start operating off the record with the mayor. This is because an issue bigger than money has arisen – the finance guy's ego. Oh, you can get your own bean counter to beat the crap out of him, but it will not do you any good. We're now talking about respect and the finance guy isn't seeing any coming from your direction. His "integrity" has been challenged and he is ready to slash your tires.

This is why it is wise to have someone to deal with and deflect the finance guy. He's a problem. If you should be so unfortunate as to be negotiating during a downturn in the business cycle, this guy is going to look like Darth Vader with a nerd pack. That mechanical pencil he wields is lethal.

As before, there is no sense going to the next step until this issue is resolved or falls off the radar. You do not need to win, you just have to wear them down until they let go.

Step Nine – Make Your Initial Proposal

If you have followed all of the previous directions, you know what your initial proposal should be. If you have skipped that part, go back to Stage 5, Steps 5 and 6.

Step Ten – Get the City's Initial Proposal

You cannot go on until the city ponies up a proposal. It has to be a legitimate proposal. What is a legitimate proposal? It is something below your walk away number, but not totally off the chart. If your bottom line is 3 percent and you believe that the city will go as high as 5 percent, an initial proposal of 1 percent by the city is within a reasonable range. A proposal of no increase or a 2 percent pay cut is a lie and a joke. Keep digging until the city comes up with a credible offer.

Step Eleven – Make Mutual Concessions

Most cities will make their initial lowball proposal and give you the ole "take-it-or-leave-it" ploy. That only works if you allow it to. Never make a counter-proposal without getting something of equal value from the city – we will come down by a half percent if you will go up a half percent. Remember, all proposals outside of the strike zone are only for show. To really have serious discussion, each side will have to move into the strike zone. Anything that gets both sides closer to that zone facilitates the process.

After a few concessions by each side, negotiations should be done in the positional mode. You can drop the pretext language (recruitment and retention), as well as the subtext (implying a pay raise without actually stating it), and be blunt and direct. The battle for the heart is over. From this point forward, it is more of a war of wills. There is nothing wrong with that.

Step Twelve – Agree or Declare Impasse

At some point, the two parties have to come to an agreement or impasse needs to be declared. Most negotiations require that the union declare impasse. It's just how the game is played.

Step Thirteen – Dump the Formal Negotiations

If you decide that impasse needs to be declared, you need to dump the formal process and proceed with the informal process. Now is when the relationships that we discussed earlier become important. If you have not developed a relationship with the mayor prior to this point, you are probably screwed. And another thing, you can forget about the legal eagles who are telling you that you cannot have off-the-record and informal talks. Just kick them in the butt; they deserve it. If you have not gained a deal by now, all of legal guy's malarkey is not going to get the job done. You have to be bold.

Step Fourteen – Go Back to the Formal Negotiations

Once you have worked the informal channel, go back to the formal negotiations to make the final deal. Just because you restart the

formal talks does not mean that the informal talks should be
suspended.

Step Fifteen – Deal with "Howard Hughes"

What if your mayor tries to barricade himself in city hall and refuses
to meet with you? Even worse, what if you believe that he is not
being briefed on what is being said at the negotiating table? This
happens quite often. It is usually done on the advice of legal guy
(the city attorney). Legal guy is so convinced that ink on paper
controls the world, he is relying on you playing by his rules. We
all know that if ink on paper controlled the world, there would be
no need for a police department. So, how do you deal with this?
You fight fire with fire. Give him ink on paper – newsprint. Begin
leaking financial data to the press. It has to be leaked. You cannot
be associated with the leak. Remember when we talked about
building a relationship with the press? Today is pay day.

I know what you are thinking. The mayor will just take the Rhett
Butler position – "Frankly, my dear, I don't give a damn." Well
frankly, he will give a damn. To maintain control of the city, the
mayor and his bureaucratic allies must always be painting a picture
of pending financial doom. Oh, finance guy is a genius when it
comes to this shell game. There are two big advantages to this ruse.
First, it preempts any insolent pretenders who might want funding
for something other than what the mayor is promoting. The second,
and best, is that by predicting a financial train wreck, the mayor
can take credit for the "save" when the wreck does not occur. This
canard is repeated year after year in virtually every city in this
country.

In addition, the mayor runs the risk of losing credibility. Obviously, lying is not a fatal defect. If it were, there would be no politicians in Washington. The ironic thing about this, is that the mayor probably does not know whether he has been lying or not when talking about the city's finances. The typical mayor in this country cannot read and comprehend his city's financial statements. He is relying totally on finance guy. Finance guy and legal guy are almost always lying. They do not see it as lying, only bluffing. Bluffing is lying. Presenting bogus predictions is lying. Preparing a budget that underestimates revenues and overstates expenditures is lying. Lying is when the words coming from your mouth do not agree with the facts in your head.

The most important thing to keep in mind is that the information has to be distributed in the form of a leak. Leaked information has much more impact. What if you get confronted about the source of the leak? Try to deflect the question by asking questions. However, under no circumstances should you deny your participation. Do not stoop to the same level as finance guy and legal guy. You can just refuse to answer the question. Sure, your refusal will probably be taken as an admission of guilt, but at least you did not lie.

Next, you should be working on the city council. I realize this is contrary to what we discussed earlier, but we are now dealing with a situation that has gone awry. There are several things that we want to accomplish. One, we want to embolden some of the council members to challenge the mayor at the same time that the press is taking him to the woodshed. Second, we want to be cultivating potential challengers for the next mayoral race. This is how we want to influence the electoral process. We want to create opportunities for candidates that could replace our recalcitrant mayor. Providing this opportunity is much more valuable than any PAC contribution or endorsement you might give. We do all of this just under the radar.

Political activities are simple – reward your friends and punish your enemies. You punish your enemies vicariously – you let someone else do it. All you need to do is create an opening for your proxy. Once you reach this point, you are probably going to have to write off the current mayor. As unpleasant as it may be, sometimes you have to be aggressive.

Step Sixteen – Get the Deal Ratified

The first step to ratification is getting 100 percent buy-in from both negotiating teams. Have a signature block for everyone on both negotiating teams. If you do not, you could have people on the team running the "Trojan Horse" play. This is where a person on the negotiating team makes no objection at the time of a tentative agreement, but later claims he did not support the agreement. Before the contract can be ratified, the tentative agreement has to be memorialized. There has to be an official copy of the redacted contract to present to the city council and the union membership. How should you go about this? First, develop a simple draft of the articles that are being changed. Next, write the final language based on that draft. Forget about all of that "know all men by these presences" baloney. The entire contract should be written in the vernacular, using short declarative sentences. Do not use legal pomp and circumstance double-talk. Make the language bomb proof. The more commas you use, the greater the chance for disputes. Do not let your attorney discuss the contract with the city's attorney. They will blow up the deal. Each will try to out-lawyer the other. It's an ego thing that attorneys have.

To get your deal done, two votes are required – the council and your membership. Get approval from your membership first. The mayor has already counted the votes on the council and knows he has a majority. Otherwise, he would not have settled with you. How about your membership? That's a whole different ball game. No matter how good a deal you have obtained, a few articulate hot heads can swing the vote to rejection. The council vote is much more reliable and less volatile.

Prepare a discussion paper that tells the provisions of the agreement. The paper should include the impact and rationale for each item. The introduction to the explanation should say that although the changes are less than what you would have liked to get, they are still more than what the city wanted to do. Say that the agreement is fair for both the city and the police officers. Send out this paper several days prior to the vote. Immediately begin a reconnaissance mission to identify those who are vocally opposing the agreement. Go to them and find out their objections firsthand. Do not engage in a debate with these people. Ask what it would take to get their support. This cannot be changes to the agreement. Even if you cannot change their minds you can at least prepare to address their objections at the union meeting.

Obviously, all of your members cannot attend a ratification meeting and some will have to vote by absentee ballot. Do not dispense with a meeting and rely entirely on absentee ballots. The meeting is the best vessel to secure the required votes. Do not be discouraged if the turnout is light. This usually means that you have the vote. It is normally those that are unhappy that make an effort to attend. Try to address the concerns of the dissidents. However, do not oversell the deal. It could get back to the council and sway some yes votes to the no column.

Finally, the council vote. Let the mayor handle this. If he insists on you speaking, be brief and use the same message that you used with your membership:

> *"This agreement is less than what we would have liked to have obtained. However, it is fair for the police officers, the department, and the city."*

Prologue

Now that you have completed the six stages, I have some final thoughts to leave you with. All negotiating circumstances will not fit exactly within the program I have given you. You will have to be able to make on-site adjustments. You may be confronted with situations that require actions that I could never have anticipated. One mistake that I see often is the demonizing of the people representing the city. I have taken some shots at them myself, especially legal guy, but keep this in mind – the people representing the city are among the decent people in your community. They are not the crackheads and gang bangers that you have to deal with on a daily basis. It is easy to fall into the trap of seeing them as villains. Treating these people with dignity and respect is not only good for negotiations, it is also the right thing to do.

Negotiations are simply you trying to convince someone else to make a change that you want – an increase in your paycheck. It is not war. It does not require anger or animosity. What is really needed is empathy. Unless you can think like the person you are attempting to influence, and you understand his point of view, you will have little chance of getting him to implement a change. All of your focus must be on the wants and needs of the other person. Do not get derailed because everything is done by proxy through a hired gun. Recognize and use protocol. Sometimes you will need to strictly adhere to it, while you may need to violate it at other times. If playing it straight is working, then continue doing so. If it is floundering, go around the normal channels. Protocol is natural law, not that legal crap that attorneys try to saddle you with.

Anger is probably your biggest enemy. A person who is mad is just as impaired as someone who is inebriated. Anger will overcome you without notice sometimes. When that occurs, take a break and end negotiations for the day. You cannot make rational decisions if your emotions are out of control.

Do not become euphoric. It only brings on depression. Sometimes it may look like you are about to hit a home run; that seldom happens. You must be bold and unpredictable, but always remain in control. Negotiations are like baseball – always have your eye on the ball. The action is always where the ball is. Watch the ball until it hits the bat. Watch the ball until it is in your glove. Stay focused on your goal. Know where the warning track (your bottom line) is at all times.

Do not let self-doubt dull your enthusiasm. When you get shot down, and you will, do not lose your confidence. I have made that mistake many times. I would go home thinking I was inept and incompetent, going over every moment that led to my rejection. Learn from your mistakes and come back using a new angle.

Rejection is not something that most of us can deal with very well. Rejection is just a part of negotiations. If you never receive rejection, you are not bold enough. When I was a firefighter, we were retiring an old fire engine. It was one of those open cab apparatuses with the steering wheel on the right side. An old retired fireman, about ninety years old, came by the station and started complaining about us getting rid of this old engine. He tried to tell us that it was the best fire truck we ever had. We started to tell him about its deficiencies - most important was the lack of pressure gauges. We asked him how he knew whether he had the correct pressure on the hose. He said there was nothing to it. You get a hose man on the nozzle and you crank up the pressure until his feet start to come off the ground. Then, you back it off just a little. That is how aggressive you need to be with your negotiations. When their feet come off the ground, don't back down completely, but give just a little bit.

You have to keep trying. If at first you do not succeed, fail, fail, and fail again. Eventually, you will succeed.

Appendix A:
Past and Current Client Listing

ARKANSAS

- Jacksonville Fraternal Order of Police

CALIFORNIA

- Arcadia Police Officers' Association
- Del Norte County Sheriff Employees Association
- Fresno County Deputy Sheriffs Association
- Fullerton Police Officers' Association
- Hanford Police Officers' Association
- Long Beach Police Officers' Association
- Ontario Police Officers' Association and the City of Ontario
- Pomona Police Officers' Association and the City of Pomona
- Whittier Police Officers' Association

COLORADO

- Adams County Fraternal Order of Police

- Arvada (Colorado Fraternal Order of Police)
- Denver Police Protective Association
- Denver Fraternal Order of Police (Sheriff Deputies)
- Englewood Police Benefit Association
- Ft. Collins (Northern Colorado Fraternal Order of Police)
- Lakewood (Colorado Fraternal Order of Police)
- Larimer County Fraternal Order of Police
- Las Animas County (Colorado Fraternal Order of Police)

CONNECTICUT

- Newington International Brotherhood of Police Officers' Local 443
- Stamford Police Association

DISTRICT OF COLUMBIA

- United States Capitol Police Labor Committee

FLORIDA

- Boca Raton Fraternal Order of Police
- Tallahassee (Big Bend Police Benevolent Association)
- Volusia County (International Brotherhood of Teamsters, Local 385)

ILLINOIS

- Chicago Fraternal Order of Police
- DeKalb County Metropolitan Alliance of Police, Chapter 318
- Rock Island (International Association of Fire Fighters, Local 26)
- Sycamore Fraternal Order of Police

INDIANA

- Indianapolis Fraternal Order of Police

KANSAS

- Dodge City Fraternal Order of Police
- Edwardsville Fraternal Order of Police
- Hays Fraternal Order of Police
- Hutchinson Fraternal Order of Police
- Hutchinson (International Association of Fire Fighters)
- Manhattan (Riley County Fraternal Order of Police)
- Kansas City Fraternal Order of Police
- Kansas Troopers' Association (state troopers)
- Lawrence Fraternal Order of Police
- Leavenworth Fraternal Order of Police
- Olathe Fraternal Order of Police
- Sedgwick County (International Association of Fire Fighters)
- Topeka Fraternal Order of Police
- Topeka (International Association of Fire Fighters)
- Wichita Fraternal Order of Police
- Wichita (International Association of Fire Fighters)
- Wyandotte County Fraternal Order of Police

KENTUCKY

- Lexington (Bluegrass Fraternal Order of Police)
- Louisville (River City Fraternal Order of Police)
- Paducah (Jackson Purchase Fraternal Order of Police)

LOUISIANA

- Alexandria Police Officers' Association
- Baton Rouge Union of Police
- Hammond Union of Police
- Lake Charles Police Officers' Association
- New Iberia Policeman's Association

MASSACHUSETTS

- Boston Police Patrolmen's Association
- Canton Police Association
- Charlton Police Alliance
- Dover Police Association
- Franklin Police Association
- Ipswich Police Officers' Association
- New Bedford Police Union
- North Attleboro Police Officers' Association
- North Attleboro Professional Police Officers' Association
- Rockport Police Association
- Saugus Police Patrol Officers' Union
- Sharon Police Association
- Westford Police Association
- Wrentham Police Association

MICHIGAN

- Kalamazoo Public Safety Officer's Association
- Kalamazoo County Sheriff's Deputies Association

MINNESOTA

- St. Paul Police Federation

MISSOURI

- Grandview Fraternal Order of Police
- Hannibal Fraternal Order of Police
- Independence Fraternal Order of Police
- Jackson County Fraternal Order of Police
- Kansas City Police Officers' Association
- Lebanon (Greater Ozark's Police Officer's Association
- Lee's Summit Fraternal Order of Police
- Liberty Fraternal Order of Police
- Pettis County Fraternal Order of Police

- Raytown Fraternal Order of Police
- Sedalia Fraternal Order of Police
- Springfield Police Officers' Association
- St. Charles Fraternal Order of Police
- St. Joseph Fraternal Order of Police
- St. Louis Fraternal Order of Police
- St. Louis County Fraternal Order of Police

MONTANA

- Missoula Police Association

NEBRASKA

- Grand Island Fraternal Order of Police
- Omaha Police Union

NEVADA

- Boulder City Police Protective Association
- Clark County Schools Police Officers' Association
- Las Vegas Police Protective Association
- North Las Vegas Police Officers' Association
- Nye County Sheriff's Deputy Officers' Association

NEW JERSEY

- Freehold Borough PBA #159

NEW MEXICO

- Albuquerque Police Officers' Association

NEW YORK

- Buffalo Police Benevolent Association
- Nassau County Detectives Association

- New York State Correctional Officers' and Police Benevolent Association, Inc.

OHIO

- Beachwood Fraternal Order of Police
- Cleveland Police Patrolmen Association
- Cleveland Fraternal Order of Police
- Fostoria (Ohio Patrolmen's Benevolent Association)
- Ohio State Trooper's Association
- Springfield Police Patrolmen's Association
- Youngstown Police Association

OKLAHOMA

- Ada Fraternal Order of Police
- Altus Fraternal Order of Police
- Bartlesville Fraternal Order of Police
- Bethany Fraternal Order of Police
- Bixby Fraternal Order of Police
- Broken Arrow Fraternal Order of Police
- Broken Arrow (International Association of Fire Fighters)
- Calera Fraternal Order of Police
- Catoosa Fraternal Order of Police
- Chickasha Fraternal Order of Police
- Choctaw Fraternal Order of Police
- Claremore Fraternal Order of Police
- Clinton Fraternal Order of Police
- Coweta Fraternal Order of Police
- Del City Fraternal Order of Police
- Duncan Fraternal Order of Police
- Durant Fraternal Order of Police
- Durant (International Association of Fire Fighters)
- Edmond Fraternal Order of Police
- El Reno Fraternal Order of Police
- Enid Fraternal Order of Police
- Guthrie Fraternal Order of Police

- Hugo Fraternal Order of Police
- Jenks Fraternal Order of Police
- McAlester Fraternal Order of Police
- Miami Fraternal Order of Police
- Midwest City Fraternal Order of Police
- Moore Fraternal Order of Police
- Muskogee Fraternal Order of Police
- Mustang Fraternal Order of Police
- Nichols Hills Fraternal Order of Police
- Noble Fraternal Order of Police
- Norman Fraternal Order of Police
- Norman (International Association of Fire Fighters)
- Oklahoma City Fire Fighters Association
- Okmulgee Fraternal Order of Police
- Okmulgee (International Association of Fire Fighters)
- Owasso Fraternal Order of Police
- Perry Fraternal Order of Police
- Ponca City Fraternal Order of Police
- Sallisaw Fraternal Order of Police
- Sand Springs Fraternal Order of Police
- Sapulpa Fraternal Order of Police
- Seminole Fraternal Order of Police
- Skiatook Fraternal Order of Police
- Stillwater Fraternal Order of Police
- Tulsa Fraternal Order of Police

OREGON

- Port of Portland Police AFSCME Local 1847

PENNSYLVANIA

- Bristol Township Police Benevolent Association
- Police Association of Falls Township
- Middletown Police Benevolent Association

SOUTH DAKOTA

- Minnehaha County Fraternal Order of Police
- Rapid City Fraternal Order of Police
- Sioux Falls Fraternal Order of Police

TENNESSEE

- Franklin Fraternal Order of Police
- Nashville Fraternal Order of Police

TEXAS

- Abilene Police Officers' Association
- Austin Police Association
- Bexar County Deputy Sheriffs Association
- Corpus Christi Police Officers' Association
- Dallas Police Association
- Denton County Fraternal Order of Police
- Department of Public Safety Officers' Association
- Jefferson County Association Of Deputy Sheriff's And Correction Officers'
- Killeen Fraternal Order of Police
- Midland Fraternal Order of Police
- Montgomery County Law Enforcement Association
- Odessa Fraternal Order of Police
- Port Arthur Police Officers' Association
- Round Rock Police Protective Association and The City Of Round Rock
- San Angelo Fraternal Order of Police

UTAH

- Salt Lake County Deputy Sheriffs Federation

VIRGINIA

- Fairfax County Coalition of Police, Local 5000

WASHINGTON

- Kennewick Police Officer's Benefit Association
- Vancouver Police Officer's Guild

WEST VIRGINIA

- Fairmont Fraternal Order of Police
- Princeton Fraternal Order of Police
- Wheeling Fraternal Order of Police

The Police Negotiator's Handbook (Discount Card)

The bearer of this card is entitled to
any applicable discounts offered by
POLICEPAY.NET to their clients.

(Do not cut your book. Please send a photocopy of
this page with your payment to receive dicounts.)

Current Discount Offers

$50 off any training event

5% off Pay Studies

5% off Ability-to-Pay Studies

5% off Turnover Reports

5% off Costing Reports

Offers are subject to change at any time. For special promotions and discounts, check our Web site regularly or call us at (405) 701-8616 today!

POLICEPAY.NET, Inc.   (405) 701-8616
219 West Boyd Street, Suite 205   (405) 701-8631
Norman, Oklahoma 73069   editor@policepay.net

WWW.POLICEPAY.NET

Lightning Source UK Ltd.
Milton Keynes UK
UKHW040705100519
342454UK00001B/323/P